# When Things Go Wrong

## Recovering from disappointments

SELWYN HUGHES

CW01046064

CWR, Waverley Abbey House, Waverley Lane, Farnham, Surrey GU9 8EP, England.

NATIONAL DISTRIBUTORS

**AUSTRALIA:** CMC Australasia, PO Box 519, Belmont,Victoria 3216.
Tel: (052) 413 288

**CANADA:** CMC Distribution Ltd., PO Box 7000, Niagara on the Lake, Ontario LOS 1JO. Tel: 1-800-325-1297

**INDIA:** Full Gospel Literature Stores, 254 Kilpauk Garden Road, Madras 600 010.
Tel: (44) 644 1353

**KENYA:** Christian Products Ltd., PO Box 56495, Nairobi.
Tel: (02) 567516

**MALAYSIA:** Salvation Book Centre (M), 23 Jalan SS2/64, Sea Park, 47300 Petaling Jaya, Selangor. Tel: (3) 7766411

**NEW ZEALAND:** CMC New Zealand Ltd., PO Box 949, 205 King Street South, Hastings. Tel: (6) 8784408

**NIGERIA:** FBFM, (Every Day with Jesus), Prince's Court, 37 Ahmed Onibudo Street, PO Box 70952, Victoria Island. Tel: 01-2617721, 616832

**REPUBLIC OF IRELAND:** Scripture Union, 40 Talbot Street, Dublin 1.
Tel: (01) 8363764

**SINGAPORE:** Campus Crusade Asia Ltd., 315 Outram Road, 06–08 Tan Boon Liat Building, Singapore 169074. Tel: (65) 222 3640

**SOUTH AFRICA:** Struik Christian Books (Pty Ltd), PO Box 193, Maitland 7405, Cape Town. Tel: (021) 551 5900

**USA:** CMC Distribution, PO Box 644, Lewiston, New York 14092-0644.
Tel: 1-800-325-1297

When Things Go Wrong

Copyright © CWR 1997

Design and Typesetting: CWR Production

Printed in Great Britain by Clifford Frost

Photographs: Corel Corporation, Photodisc

ISBN 1 85345 113 4

Material originally published in EDWJ

Unless otherwise identified, all Scripture quotations in this publication are from the Holy Bible: New International Version (NIV). Copyright © 1973, 1978, 1984, International Bible Society.

# Introduction

The theme for this special series brims over with hope and confidence – a hope and confidence that are so much needed in those times when we are called to walk in darkness.

The secret of *why* God chooses to lead us into the darkness is revealed to us in Isaiah 45:3 *"I will give you the treasures of darkness, riches stored in secret places, so that you may know that I am the Lord."* There are treasures which can only be found in the dark. John Bunyan found them in the darkness of a prison and wrote the immortal *Pilgrim's Progress.* Helen Keller, blind and deaf, found treasures in her darkness and shared them with the world through her glowing spirit. In a deep dark well you can look up and see the stars, even when people in the light above cannot see them. We can discover treasures in the darkness that we would never be able to find in the light.

When we find ourselves surrounded by darkness we must look for the meaning that lies within it. Many Christians allow the darkness to drag their spirits down to such a degree that they lose their faith. They do not know how to search out the treasures that lay all around them.

When Jesus took upon Himself our flesh He deliberately and voluntarily limited Himself to finding out about life in the way we find out – by grappling with issues day after day. He learned about the treasure that is in the darkness of suffering.

We are not going to be exempt from the difficult periods of life just because we are Christians. If we have this attitude it will hinder us from discovering the treasures that are all around. Periods of darkness can be times of great spiritual advance providing we stand up to them with the right attitude which says that God will allow nothing to come into my life unless it can be used.

The apostle Paul found grace in the darkness of a prison experience and when our souls are open to that grace which constantly flows towards us from heaven then every difficult situation can be the setting for a new discovery of God and a new revelation of His love.

If at this moment you find yourself in darkness and your heart is broken and dispirited, then give God all the broken pieces and allow Him to put your life together again, perhaps in a new and more glorious pattern.

In this booklet we dig for the treasures to be found in the darkness of disappointment. When things go wrong in our lives it can be one of the most difficult periods of life. Everything is thrown into confusion but treasures can be found here. We look particularly at shattered hopes and plans, financial failure and broken relationships.

# Shattered Hopes
## and Plans

# Shattered hopes and plans

One form of darkness in which God invites us to take the pickaxe of faith and dig for meaning is the darkness of shattered hopes and plans. I have no doubt that many read-

*"Then all the people ... asked Jesus to leave them, because they were overcome with fear."*

ing these lines are there right now. The time when all our plans seem to go wrong is one of the most difficult periods of life. It throws confusion into everything for so much can be geared to those plans. But listen carefully to me – there are treasures to be found even in this deep darkness.

Look with me at how Jesus reacted to the blocking of His plans in the incident that is before us. After He had healed the man possessed with devils, the people came to see what had happened and found the man "sitting at Jesus' feet, dressed and in his right mind" (v.35). The passage goes on to say, "and they were afraid". Afraid of what? They were afraid of something they could not understand. They could handle insanity better than they could handle sanity. Insanity was familiar to them, but the deliverance of the demonic was something very unfamiliar. So they begged Jesus to leave.

*For further thought*

**Luke 3:1–6; Isa. 40:4, 45:2; Matt. 16:18**

1. What was prophesied of Jesus?

2. What did Jesus declare?

How did Jesus react to this apparent blocking of His ministry in that region? He turned in another direction and when you read the next two chapters you find one astonishing miracle after another. He turned the blocking into a blessing. If He couldn't do this, He could do that. The frustration turned to fruitfulness. So when your plans are upset do what Jesus did – utilise the grace that flows from God and prepare to turn in another direction.

# Isolation becomes revelation

We have seen how opposition did not deter Jesus but deflected Him, and resulted in a spate of astonishing miracles: the deflection became a spur. There are treasures to be found in every difficulty, a dawn in every midnight, opportunities in every opposition. Am I talking now to someone whose plans have been completely overturned? Maybe you are sitting reading these lines feeling as if the world has caved in on you. Lift up your heart – the eternal God has a word for you. His grace and power are flowing towards you at this very moment, and if you avail yourself of them, then the block can become a blessing, the frustration can be turned into fruitfulness, and the setback become a stepping stone.

**Revelation 1:4–20**

*"I, John ... was on the island of Patmos because of the word of God and the testimony of Jesus."* (v.9)

When John found himself on the Isle of Patmos, incarcerated for the sake of the Gospel, it must have seemed that his ministry and all his plans had been rudely shattered. He says, "I, John ... found myself in the island called Patmos, for adhering to God's word and the testimony of Jesus" (1:9, Moffatt). However, he continues: "On the Lord's day I found myself rapt in the Spirit, and I heard a loud voice ... calling, 'Write your vision ...'" (vv.10–11). Isolated, and prevented from preaching the Gospel, he wrote a book that has blessed men and women down the centuries. The place of isolation became a place of revelation.

*For further thought*

**Hab. 1, 2:1–3**

1. What was Habakkuk's complaint?

2. What was God's response?

This is what can happen to you if you do not allow yourself to sink into self-pity and instead receive the grace that God is offering you now. Sit down amongst your broken and shattered plans and "write out" the vision of the new and better ones that God will give you.

# Working with a wound

**Matthew 14:1–14**

We continue focusing on the thought that when our present plans are shattered God can enable us to build bigger and better ones. But remember that this treasure comes only to those who dig – dig for meaning and understanding.

*"When Jesus heard what had happened, he withdrew by boat privately to a solitary place ... the crowds followed him ..."*
*(v.13)*

Look at the picture before us. Jesus had just heard that John the Baptist, His cousin and forerunner, had been beheaded. The account says: "When Jesus heard it, he withdrew by boat to a desert place in private" (v.13, Moffatt). No doubt the Saviour longed to be alone with His grief, but verse 13 continues, "but the crowds heard of it and followed him on foot from the towns." They broke up His plans. Now what did Jesus do? Did He turn on the people and reprimand them for invading His privacy? Listen again to what the account says: "So when he disembarked, he saw a large crowd, and out of pity for them he healed their sick folk" (v.14, Moffatt). He turned His hurt into healing and responded to the situation with infinite tenderness and compassion. Our Lord had a wound in His heart but that wound became healing for others.

Now you may think that it is insensitive of me to talk about ministry to others when you are hurting, but this is precisely what you need to hear. I am not unmindful of the hurt you go through when important plans are thwarted, but if self-pity is to be challenged and your life turned in a new direction, you must let me tell you in the most loving way I can that your wound can become healing for others. The same Lord who ministered with a wound in His heart can both minister to you and through you. Oh I pray that you may feel His touch at this very moment – this very hour.

*For further thought*

**Acts 20:25–35; Eccl.11:1; Matt. 10:8; Luke 6:38**

1. What is it more blessed to do?

2. What is God's way of working?

# "The show will go on"

We are seeing that there are treasures to be found in every period of darkness – even the darkness of shattered hopes and plans. Someone has spoken of "getting meaning out of

**Psalm 62:1–12**

*"He alone is my rock and my salvation; he is my fortress, I shall never be shaken." (v.2)*

life's remainders". Sometimes life leaves us with nothing but "remainders". Everything we longed for has gone and we are left with just "remainders" which are nothing more than reminders of what might have been. But what I am saying is this – we can get meaning out of those "remainders". "A Christian," says Billy Graham, "is someone who, when he or she comes to the end of a rope, ties a knot and holds on." Are you at the end of a rope at this moment? Then take his advice – tie a knot and hang on.

There is a passage in the book of Revelation that says, "... there was silence in heaven for about half an hour" (Rev. 8:1). I heard a preacher say, "That was because God was moving the scenery for the next act." Can you dare believe that in the period when important plans have broken up God is at work moving the scenery for the next act? Hold steady – the show will go on. In the meantime, prepare to let God give you the assurance that there is a point and a purpose to what has happened to you. Let the "remainders" be your reminders that with God all things are possible.

*For further thought*

**Mark 10:17–27;**
**Matt. 17:20, 19:26;**
**Luke 1:37, 18:27**

1. What did Jesus declare to the disciples?

2. What is He saying to you?

I met a man some time ago who told me that a year earlier his plans to emigrate and start a new life with his family had been overturned just a few days before he was due to leave the country. "I thought life had come to an end," he told me, "but within weeks God moved me into an exciting new career that hitherto I could not have dreamed was possible." The upset served only to set him up.

# The hidden "better"

How it must have upset the plans of the disciples when they were told by Jesus that He was about to leave them! After three years it seemed His ministry was just beginning to make its mark and their hearts must have sunk within them as they heard Him say: "I am soon about to leave you." What a sense of spiritual orphanage must have stolen across their hearts: they would be left alone in the world without Him. Those disciples, remember, had given up their jobs to travel with Him. Peter had turned from his fishing nets, Matthew from his tax collecting, and so on. Our Lord's announcement that He was soon to go away must have sounded like a thunder clap in their souls. It was the collapse of all their hopes and expectations.

**John 16:5–16**

*"In a little while you will see me no more, and then after a little while you will see me."*
(v.16)

However, His going brought them an even greater blessing. Our text puts it most beautifully when it says: "It is for your good that I am going away" (v.7). In effect, Jesus was saying something like this: "I will take away My physical presence but instead you will experience My omnipresence. I will be closer to you than I have ever been before. The Holy Spirit will bring Me back, not just to be alongside, but within you. You will just have to drop into the recesses of your own heart and I will be there – burningly, blessedly there."

*For further thought*

**John 15:18–27; Acts 1:4–8, 2:1–4**

1. What did Jesus promise to the disciples?

2. What would have happened if they had gone home after the Ascension?

The disciples were to learn, as you and I must learn, that God never takes away the good unless He plans to replace it with the better. After Pentecost, the disciples must have said to each other: "It is true He has gone, but somehow He is closer to us than ever." Oh, if only we could learn that the shattering of our plans is but the prelude to the advancement of His!

# Shattered Hopes and Plans

Facing shattered hopes and the crumbling of life's plans can be a desolate and paralysing darkness.

Allow God to come alongside you, like John on the Isle of Patmos; ask Him to give you the guidance and strength you need to "write out" your personal vision, and that He might help you see that the break up of your present plans can lead to bigger and better ones. Also that this place of "isolation" might become, as it did for John, a place of "revelation".

Be comforted that Jesus winced too when He was wounded and He went on to use His wounds to reach out to others. Ask Him now to heal your wounds and that your wounds might heal someone else's.

Can we dare to believe also that the silence from heaven is "God moving the scenery for the next act"? Hold steady as God makes a new way for you.

Finally as you read these pages ask that God might give you a resilient spirit and that He would give you the strength not to be deterred by the blocking of your plans and that by His grace He will make new and better ones. So that we too can join with the Psalmist and say "he is my fortress, I shall never be shaken".

# Financial Failure

# When money takes wings

We now focus on another form of darkness – the darkness of financial failure or material loss. Dare we believe that God can help us find treasure when there has been a financial catastrophe? Well, once again I say – He can!

**Proverbs 23:1–8**

*"Do not wear yourself out to get rich ... Cast but a glance at riches, and they are gone, for they will surely sprout wings ..." (vv. 4–5)*

Many years ago I had a friend who suffered a serious financial reverse and lost everything – literally everything. He came out of it, however, with a philosophy of life that enabled him to say: "Never again will I be broken by material loss." And why? Because out of his downfall he built a biblical framework which enabled him to see the whole issue of finance from God's perspective. He has come back now from bankruptcy and is once again a wealthy man, but this time around he holds his possessions more loosely and sees himself, not as a proprietor, but as a steward. You see, it sometimes takes an upset to set us up, in the sense that we do not gain the right perspective on things until we are brought down into a crisis.

*For further thought*

**Deut. 8:1–18;
1 Chron. 29:12;
Eccl. 5:19**

1. What was the admonition to the Israelites?

2. What were they to remember?

Do you find yourself this moment in a financial reverse? Have you been stripped of many, if not all, of your assets? Then take careful note of the meditations that follow for I want to share with you some principles that will help to rebuild your life and bring you into a deeper understanding than ever before of the biblical purpose of possessions. This also applies to those who may not at this moment be in reduced financial circumstances because in a world such as this a financial reverse can come at any time. It behoves us all to learn how to live independently of our possessions because one day we may be called upon to do just that.

# Transferring ownership

The first thing we must get straight about the whole issue of money and possessions is that in themselves they are not evil. Some Christians speak scornfully of those who have a good deal of money. The Bible never does that. It brings to task those who make

**Genesis 22:1–19**

*"... because you have done this and have not withheld your son, your only son, I will surely bless you ..."*
*(vv. 16–17)*

money their god, but it never rails against money as such. So, see clearly that money in itself is not evil; it lends itself to a thousand philanthropies, feeds the hungry, clothes the naked, succours the destitute and through it many errands of mercy are performed. It is true that money cannot bring happiness, but as someone said, "It can certainly put our creditors in a better frame of mind."

Whether you have a little or a lot of this world's goods, I suggest that if you have never taken the following step, then you do it now – *in a definite act of commitment, transfer the ownership of all your possessions into the hands of God.* Those of you who have been stripped of everything will need to do this as an act of faith, indicating that should God ever allow you to have possessions again, you will see yourself as a steward and not a proprietor. The friend to whom I referred previously – the one who lost everything – told me that after reading the passage which is before us, he got on his knees and by faith said to God: "Whatever comes into my hands again, I will hold in trust for You." That act of dedication became the point of transformation. God took him at his word and helped him rebuild his life.

*For further thought*

**Matt. 25:14–30; 1 Cor. 4:2; Rom. 14:12**

1. What is required of a steward?

2. What were "talents"?

If in reality we do not own anything, but are given things from God, then the common-sense thing is to say: "Lord, I'm not the owner, but the ower." We must never forget that.

# Hitched to a plough

Once we have transferred ownership of all our possessions and material assets to God – what then? Next we should *streamline our lives for the purposes of God's Kingdom.*

**Colossians 3:1–17**

*"Set your minds on things above, not on earthly things." (v.2)*

David Livingstone once said: "I will place no value on anything that I have or possess except in relation to the Kingdom of Christ. If anything I have will advance that Kingdom, it shall be given or kept, whichever will best promote the glory of Him to whom I owe all my hopes, both for time and eternity."

Commenting on Livingstone's words, one writer said: "That first sentence of Livingstone's should become the life motto of every Christian. Each of us should repeat it slowly to ourselves every day: 'I will place no value on anything I have or possess except in relation to the

Kingdom of Christ.' If it advances the Kingdom it has value – if it is useless to the Kingdom it is valueless.

In the days when missionaries were able to work in China, John Wanamaker, a Christian businessman, who visited that country in order to see that the donations of people were being used wisely and to the best advantage, tells this story. One day he came to a village where there was a beautiful little church. In a nearby field he caught sight of a young man yoked to an ox, ploughing a field. He went over and asked the reason for this strange sight. An old man who was guiding the plough from behind said: "When we were trying to build our church, my son and I had no money to give. My son said: 'Let us sell one of our two oxen and I will take its yoke.' We did so and were able to give the money we made towards the building of the church." Wanamaker wept!

*For further thought*

**1 Kings 17:7–24;**
**Matt. 26:7;**
**2 Cor. 8:3–5**

1. What was the experience of the widow of Zarephath?

2. What did Paul testify of the saints in Macedonia?

# "Above all distinctions"

A third principle of rebuilding after a financial catastrophe is this – *learn what it means to be free to use either poverty or plenty*. History shows that as a rule people try to defend themselves against financial disaster in one of two ways. One is by saving as much as possible, and the other is by renouncing all interest in money or material things. If, in building

**Philippians 4:4–13**

*"... I have learned the secret of being content in any and every situation ... whether living in plenty or in want."*
*(v. 12)*

up financial reserves, people allow their trust and confidence to be focused on amassing riches and material possessions rather than on God, they become as metallic as the coins they seek. They are in bondage to material gain. But the other type of person can be in bondage, too, for washing one's hands of material things shows a bondage, not to riches, but to poverty.

The person who is only free to use plenty is bound by that, and the person who is only free to use poverty is bound by that. Both are in bondage. But the person who, like Paul in the text before us, has learned the secret of being content whether living in plenty or in want, experiences a true freedom.

*For further thought*

**Luke 3:1–14;**
**Prov. 15:16;**
**1 Tim. 6:6–8; Heb. 13:5**

1. What did John the Baptist say to the soldiers?

2. What was Paul's word to Timothy?

I remember reading the story of a missionary in India who got into conversation with a high caste Indian at a remote railway station. "Are you travelling on the next train?" asked the missionary. "No," replied the Indian, "the train has only third class carriages. It's all right for you, because you are a Christian and you are above such distinctions."

"Above such distinctions" – that is true Christian living. Third class doesn't degrade us and first class doesn't exalt us. Hallelujah!

# Staying on course

We look at one more principle which can help us rebuild our lives when overtaken by a financial disaster – *learn to differentiate between a need and a want.* But what are needs? And how do we differentiate between our needs, and our

**2 Corinthians 1:12–23**

*"... we have conducted ourselves in the world ... not according to worldly wisdom but according to God's grace." (v. 12)*

wants and desires? Someone has defined a need like this: "We need as much as will make us physically, mentally and spiritually fit for the purposes of God, and anything beyond that belongs to the needs of others." If this is true, then how do we decide what belongs to our needs and what belongs to the needs of others? I wish I could answer that, but it is a matter that each of us must work out between ourselves and God. Go over your life in God's presence and see what belongs to your needs and what really comes under the category of wants.

"But," someone may say, "what about luxuries – things we don't really need but which make life more pleasant?"

*For further thought*

**Phil. 4:10–20;
Isa. 58:11; Psa. 1**

1. What has God promised to supply?

2. What is a condition of prosperity?

Again, these things must be worked out in prayer between yourself and God. Only the Holy Spirit can sensitise our consciences and tune us to His purposes for our lives, and each of us may come out with different conclusions.

A fisherman said: "Some time ago I was on a lake. I pulled in my oars and let the boat drift. As I looked at the surrounding water I could see no drift at all, and only as I looked at a fixed point on the shore could I see how far I was drifting." The story is a parable. If you look around to see what others are doing and merely follow them, you will have no sense of drift. Only as you keep your eyes on Christ and remain fixed on Him will you know whether you are staying on God's course – or drifting from it.

# Financial Failure

The darkness of financial failure is often confusing and it's difficult at times to find the way forward.

Invite the Holy Spirit to help you to know what it is to be "content in any and every situation". Even though it seems impossible, our God is the God of the impossible, and as God taught Paul to be content, He is equally committed to you also. Allow Jesus to release you from being entangled by plenty or broken by poverty.

Ask your Father in Heaven to come alongside you and fill you with the faith of Abraham to believe that all things are in His hands, that you will find peace in His everlasting arms.

Take time to settle the whole area of possessions with God, be aware that our discipleship does not rest on what we own but rather on what we owe. Lay all that you have on God's altar, acknowledging that it's no longer yours but His.

Finally, invite Jesus to sensitise your spirit to hear His voice in everything you do, knowing that sometimes it takes "an upset to set us up". Explore with the Father the difference between a want and a need.

# Broken
# Relationships

# "More to follow"

We move on now to consider a form of darkness that can be filled with deep trauma – the darkness of broken relationships. I doubt whether there is any person reading these lines who has not in one way or another experienced the hurt that comes from a broken relationship. At this very moment some of you will be going through traumatic experiences, perhaps the discovery of infidelity by a marriage partner, or a separation, a divorce, a rift between parents and children, or a broken engagement or friendship. Out of loyalty to their families, many face the world with a smile, but inwardly they are torn and bleeding.

Whatever the specifics of the situation, any rift in a relationship can be a deeply wounding experience. Are there treasures to be found in the darkness of a broken relationship? If you are in this kind of situation at present, it may be difficult for you to believe that you can come through spiritually enriched, but I want to assure you that you can. A little patient "digging" in the darkness that surrounds you can yield the most priceless treasures.

"How?" I hear you ask – *"How?"* First, remind yourself that God provides sufficient grace and strength for us to deal with every situation that comes our way. You are not the first to be in this situation; others have been there and have proved that God gives grace upon grace. An anonymous

**2 Corinthians 9:1–15**

*"And God is able to make all grace abound to you ..."* (v.8)

*For further thought*

**Psa. 55; Heb. 12:25–29; 2 Cor. 4:18**

1. What caused David deep distress?

2. Where must we fix our eyes?

donor sent a poor man a £5 note every week with the message: "This is yours; use it wisely, there is more to follow." God does something similar with His grace. Every time you receive it there is always a note attached that says: "more to follow".

# A searching question

We continue taking up the pickaxe of faith to explore some of the treasures that are to be found in the darkness of broken relationships. Keep in mind that these treasures are only found as you dig for them. They don't just appear out of nowhere; they have to be searched for – with diligence, patience and trust.

**Psalm 139:13–24**

*"See if there is any offensive way in me, and lead me in the way everlasting." (v. 24).*

Once you have reminded yourself that God provides "grace upon grace", you should then face this question with courage and determination: "How much may I have contributed to the problem?" In the midst of your pain, this might be a difficult thing for you even to consider, and if you can't, don't worry – when the pain subsides you can come back to this question. But whether you do it now or later, keep in mind that face it you must. Our tendency whenever we are hurt is to see ourselves as a victim and forget that we may have contributed in some way to the problem. It may well be that you are an innocent victim but be ready and willing, nevertheless, to see if there is any way in which you may have contributed to the difficulties.

If, in looking at yourself, you find there are things that you are responsible for, then confess these things to God

*For further thought*

**1 Cor. 11:23–32;
Lam. 3:40; 2 Cor. 13:5;
Gal. 6:4**

1. What was Paul's exhortation to the Corinthians?

2. What are we to test?

and ask His forgiveness. This action will help you make a clearer and more objective assessment of the situation. Now, if you discover that you have hurt others, don't go running to them right away to ask for their forgiveness. You will need to know God's timing in this. It is always right to ask forgiveness of those we have hurt, but if it is not done at the right time it can create a wrong impression – they may, for example, feel that you are doing it to gain an advantage over them.

# In whom do we trust?

I hope you were able to see the point and purpose of what I said in the previous meditation. If we go *at the wrong time* to ask forgiveness of someone for something we have done, the action can hinder rather than help the situation.

**Psalm 56:1–13**

*"When I am afraid, I will trust in you."* (v. 3)

A woman whose husband left her took the first two steps I have suggested: first, she reminded herself that God was with her and, second, she faced with great courage the possibility that in some way she may have contributed to the problem. She asked God for His forgiveness and then immediately went searching for her husband to ask for *his* forgiveness. He interpreted this as manipulation and was not ready to receive it. Instead of drawing him to her, it drove him further away. We must be strong enough and trustful enough to await God's timing in all situations.

This brings me to my next suggestion – learn how to become a truly secure person. The secret of living successfully in this world is to remember that we are designed by God to draw our security as persons primarily from Him and not from our earthly relationships. Most of us get this wrong and draw our life from our horizontal relationships – the people around us, family, friends and so on – rather than from our vertical relationship with God. And we never know how flimsy that vertical relationship is until the horizontal relationships in which we are involved fall apart. Many have told me that they never realised how dependent they were on others until the others were no longer there; then they were devastated. We are to enter into earthly relationships and enjoy them, but we are never to be dependent on them for our life. We are to be dependent only on God.

*For further thought*

**Psa. 118:1–8, 37:5;**
**Isa. 26:4, 2:22**

1. What must we stop doing?

2. What is it better to do?

# In God we trust

If there is one thing that is clear about the whole area of relationships, it is this – relationships can hurt. A friend of mine says: "God calls us to relate to people who are guaranteed to hurt us and fail us."

**Psalm 91:1–16**

*"He who dwells in the shelter of the Most High ... will say of the Lord, 'He is my refuge and my fortress ...' " (vv. 1–2)*

This is why we must find a source of security that is not in people, but in God, the unfailing One. This does not mean that we must withdraw from people, but that we do not use them as the source of our life. Once we see that

God, and God alone, is our true security, then when earthly relationships fail we are shaken but not shattered. There is a five foot drop and not a thousand foot drop.

Let me tell you how secure people will behave when engulfed in the darkness of broken relationships. Having reminded themselves of the fact that God's grace is ever sufficient, and having looked at any way in which they may have contributed to the difficulty, and thrown themselves in utter dependency upon God, they will be strong enough to sit back and wait for God to show them exactly what to do. They will not act precipitately because they are no longer dependent on their earthly relationships to hold them together but are dependent on God. They will move with poise and prayerful determination into the situation. They know that there is no guarantee that poise and prayerful determination will bring about a resolution of the problem, but having done what God wants them to do, they are able to relax and leave the outcome to Him.

*For further thought*

**Psa. 13, 33, 21:7, 32:10, 36:7**

1. What was the psalmist convinced of?

2. Where was his trust?

Once you have moved your point of dependency from the horizontal to the vertical, and are following God's direction and guidance in all things, then, though you may still hurt, you will not be destroyed.

# The priceless pearl

Once we settle for the fact that when we draw our security directly from Christ, and not from our earthly relationships, we may still get hurt but not destroyed – then we have dis-

**Psalm 112:1–10**

*"Even in darkness light dawns for the upright ..." (v.4)*

covered one of the most priceless treasures in the universe. Unfortunately, many do not find this treasure except in the darkness of broken relationships. Like Isaiah, they do not see the glory and sufficiency of the One on the throne until they go through an experience that seems like death. "In the year that King Uzziah died, I saw the Lord ..." (Isaiah 6:1).

Some broken relationships can be healed, but some cannot. Our part is to ensure that we do everything we can to restore them and then leave the matter in God's hands. If restoration comes, then fine, but if not, providing we are open all the time to doing what God wants us to do, then God will continue to bless us, even though the relationship is not restored.

I know many Christians who are caught up at this very

*For further thought*

**Heb. 12:1–15; Rom. 13:8; Lev. 19:18**

1. What must we be careful not to miss?

2. What must we not seek?

moment in broken relationships and unhappy home situations and I observe them day by day doing what the oyster does when it gets an irritating grain of sand in its shell – they form a pearl around the problem. Just as the oyster down there in the darkness of the ocean builds a pearl around an irritant, so will God enable you to throw around all your difficult situations, especially broken relationships, a priceless pearl of character. The darkness then becomes a trysting place where daily you and the Lord work things out in ways that glorify His name. And had the darkness not come, you might never have discovered the treasure.

# Broken Relationships

There is no doubt that the darkness of broken relationships can be deeply wounding and isolating. However, pause for a moment and ask your Father not only to supply you with His grace, but to overwhelm you, that you might be a living example that He gives "grace upon grace".

Invite Jesus to help you draw strength from Him, developing a relationship that is first and foremost vertical then reaching out horizontally to others around us. So that when your earthly relationships fail, you will be receiving your life from One who can never fail.

During the times when darkness tries to overtake you, pause to consider that if God is our source when earthly relationships fail, we may be shaken but not shattered. God has promised to be our "refuge and fortress".

Spend some time considering that our God is faithful, the unfailing One who will never let you be overrun or destroyed. He cannot and will never change His commitment and love towards you. (As far as the east is from the west.)

Remember that "God is able to make all grace abound to you".

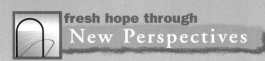

## fresh hope through
# New Perspectives

Difficult circumstances, particularly prolonged ones, can easily cause us to lose sight of God's perspective on our situation. New Perspectives aims to help people gain fresh strength and encouragement by seeing their circumstances in the light of God's Word and the grace He makes available. Thirty, easy to digest, daily readings gently unfold helpful Scriptures, practical insights and ideas for reflection and action.

### A PLACE OF REST
Dr Bill & Frances Munro give practical advice on reducing stress.
1853451010

### TODAY'S GRACE*
Frank Gamble shares an inspirational lifeline to all suffering from long-term illness. 1853451061

### BREAKTHROUGH TO LOVE
David & Maureen Brown share valuable insights for building a better marriage.
1853451029

### DOORWAY TO HOPE*
Helena Wilkinson offers fresh hope for those in despair. 1853451088

### TOWARDS THE LIGHT
Dr Ruth Fowke offers experienced help for those going through depression.
1853451002

### FINDING THE BALANCE*
Keith Tondeur provides practical advice on dealing with financial crisis.
185345107X

### STRENGTH TO CARE
Hilary Vogel provides much-needed encouragement for carers. 1853451037

### A WAY FORWARD*
Peter Curran gives encouraging help following redundancy.
1853451096

*Previously published under different titles.

96 pages   198 x 120 mm   Illustrated in colour   £4.95 each (UK)

Available from Christian bookshops or by post from National Distributors or CWR's UK distributors STL – Tel: 0345 413500 (local rate call).